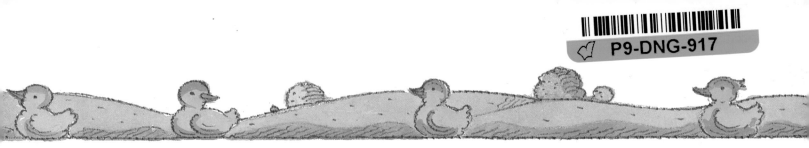

For Emma

Bill Martin Jr, Ph.D., has devoted his life to the education of
young children. Bill Martin Books reflect his philosophy: that
children's imaginations are opened up through the play of language,
the imagery of illustrations, and the permanent joy of reading books.

Illustrations copyright © 1992 by Ian Beck
All rights reserved, including the right to reproduce this book or portions thereof in any form.
Published by Henry Holt and Company, Inc., 115 West 18th Street, New York, New York 10011.
Originally published in the United Kingdom by Orchard Books.
ISBN 0-8050-2525-1

Printed in Belgium
1 3 5 7 9 10 8 6 4 2

Five Little
DUCKS

·IAN·BECK·

A Bill Martin Book

Henry Holt and Company · New York

Five little ducks went swimming one day,
Over the hills and far away.

Mother duck said, "Quack, quack, quack, quack."
But only four little ducks came back.

Four little ducks went swimming one day,
Over the hills and far away.

Mother duck said, "Quack, quack, quack, quack."
But only three little ducks came back.

Three little ducks went swimming one day,
Over the hills and far away.

Mother duck said, "Quack, quack, quack, quack."
But only two little ducks came back.

Two little ducks went swimming one day,

Over the hills and far away.

Mother duck said, "Quack, quack, quack, quack."
But only one little duck came back.

One little duck went swimming one day,

Over the hills

and far away.

Mother duck said, "Quack, quack, quack, quack."

And all her five little ducks came back.

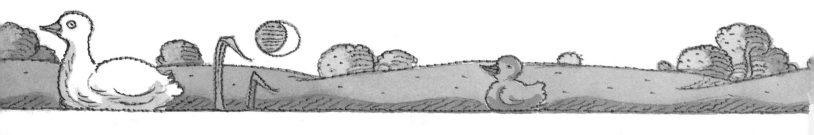